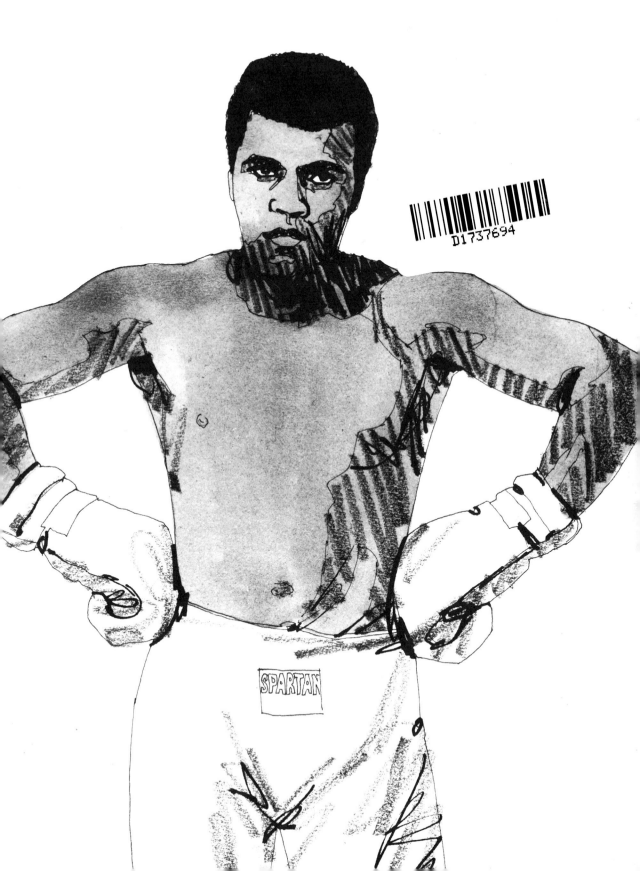

D1737694

SPARTAN

Text copyright © 1974 by Educreative Systems, Inc. Illustrations copyright © 197
by Creative Education. International copyrights reserved in all countries. No part o
this book may be reproduced in any form without written permission from th
publisher. Printed in the United States.

Library of Congresss Number: 73-10367   ISBN: O-87191-262-7

Published by Creative Education, Mankato, Minnesota 56001
Prepared for the Publisher by Educreative Systems, Inc.
Distributed by Childrens Press, 1224 West Van Buren Street, Chicago, Illinois 606

Library of Congress Cataloging in Publication Data
Educreative Systems, inc.
   I am the greatest.
   SUMMARY: A biography of a prizefighter whose dreams were realized when a
twenty-two he became heavyweight champion of the world.
   1. Muhammad Ali, 1942-   —Juvenile literature. [1. Muhammad Ali, 1942
      2. Boxing—Biography] I. Title. GV1132.M84E38 796.8'3'0924
[B] [92] 73-10367 ISBN 0-87191-262-7

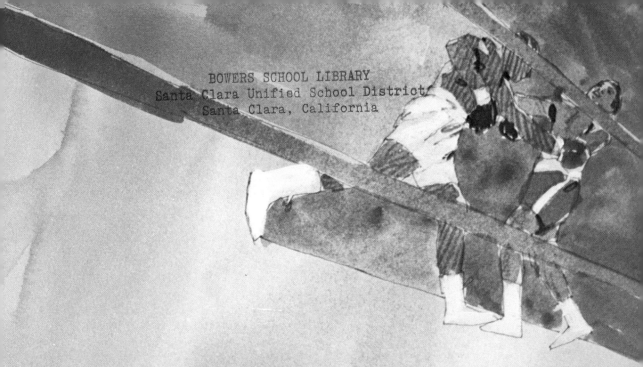

BOWERS SCHOOL LIBRARY
Santa Clara Unified School District
Santa Clara, California

MUHAMMAD ALI

"I AM THE GREATEST"

By James T. Olsen

Illustrated by Harold Henriksen

A big white apartment—across the street from Churchill Downs. Inside one of the apartments a woman was lying on the floor kicking her legs in the air. She was doing exercises. A four year old boy walked up the stairs and laid down next to her. He began to exercise too. The woman's name—Odessa Clay. The 4 year old boy—Cassius Marcellus Clay Jr.

Cassius Clay grew up to be famous all over the world as Muhammad Ali—Boxer. Ali is not the boxing champion of the world. He once was! But he is, both in his own eyes and in the eyes of many other people in America, "the greatest".

It was always that way for Ali. Even growing up as a boy in Lexington, Kentucky Cassius liked to be "the greatest" at whatever he did. For example, he would never take the bus to school. He would run along next to the bus. The children on the bus laughed.

But Cassius didn't care. He showed he could easily keep up with the bus—and sometimes even outrace it. As you might guess, Cassius also got to be a very good runner.

Cassius started to work out as a fighter in Joe Martin's gym when he was twelve years old. He didn't have time to fool around with the other kids. "Kids used to throw rocks and stand under the streetlights," he said about his childhood. "But there wasn't nothing to do in the streets. I tried it a little bit, but wasn't nothing else to do but the boxing." He learned everything he could about boxing but he wouldn't always listen to advice from other boxers or trainers. He liked his way of doing things the best. Within six weeks of stepping inside the gym Cassius won his first amateur fight! Asked who helped him most at that time he said, "I did the most for me." Within a year he was fighting amateur fights on T.V.

Cassius had decided that boxing was to be his life because that was how he would succeed. "I started boxing because I thought this was the fastest way for a black person to make it in this country. I was not that bright in school. I couldn't be a football or basketball player cause you have to go to college and get all kinds of degrees and pass examinations. A boxer can just go to a gym, jump around, turn professional, win a fight, get a break, and he is in the ring. If he's good

enough he makes more money than ball players make all their lives.

Perhaps Cassius felt more strongly about his future than most 12 year olds. He was the son of a black sign painter in Kentucky in the 1950's and life didn't promise to be easy or successful.

Once when Ali talked about growing up he said "I used to lay awake scared thinking about somebody getting cut up or lynched. I always wanted to do something to help these people. But I was too little. Maybe now I can help by living up to what I'm supposed to be . . . I guess I want people to be proud of me."

Ali's mother had a different dream for her son. "My mother always wanted me to be something like a doctor or a lawyer. Maybe I'd a made a good lawyer. I talk so much. I guess I get that from my father," he said. Cassius Clay Sr. is a tiny, quick man. He has always loved to talk and clown and yell.

Cassius did manage to graduate from high school in Louisville. By then he had fought 180 amateur fights and he had won six state Golden Glove tournaments in Kentucky. After graduation he flew to Rome, Italy for the 1960 Olympics. There, as a 178 lb. light heavyweight, he won a Gold Medal. He was the hero of the day. Winning a gold medal spread his fame outside of boxing circles.

While in Rome a Russian newsman told Cassius that his gold medal wouldn't buy him a seat in a Southern restaurant. Cassius answered, "At least I ain't fighting alligators and living in a mud hut." When Cassius returned home he painted the front stoop red, white and blue and he was given a party that "crippled the town." He was ready to turn pro—at the age of eighteen! He had a lot of physical advantages. He was 6 feet 2½ inches, over 200 lbs., had a very long reach, big arm muscles and quick, "dancing feet." His boxing method has always been to hit and not be hit.

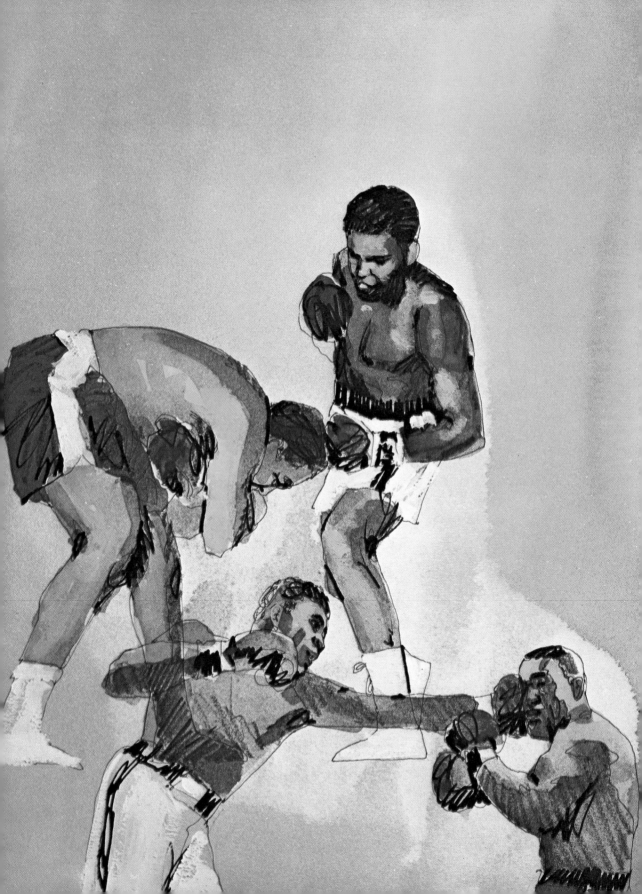

As a pro Cassius attracted a large following. He was fast, very fast. He could duck, bob, weave, moving all the time. He moved like a fast sports car does. And his punch could "sting like a bee." But Cassius has always been more than a boxer. He's a talker, too. In the ring, Cassius would make jokes and recite his own poetry. He would also insult the man he was fighting. He would make up things like:

"He thinks he is a bear,

But I know he is nowhere."

After beating Archie Moore, he finally decided to go out after Heavyweight Champion Sonny Liston. On February 25, 1964, they finally met. When the bell for the seventh round sounded, Liston was unable to come out of his corner. And at that moment, Cassius was the new Champion. He was twenty-two years of age and he was on top of the world. His dreams had come true. He was THE HEAVYWEIGHT CHAMP-ION OF THE WORLD.

The very next day, after the fight, Cassius announced that he had become a member of the Black Muslim Religion. He said the Muslims taught him good things about black people. Things he had never heard before. He said he would live by the Muslim rules. He wanted to be known by a Muslim name. He was no longer to be called Cassius Clay. His new name would be Muhammad Ali.

Many people were afraid of Muslims. Many cities would not allow Ali to fight there. Little did Ali realize that he was about to fight what would probably be the biggest fight of his life.

The U.S. Army wanted Cassius Clay. His draft classification was changed to 1-A and he had to report for a physical right away. Ali wasn't happy about that. As he said later, "For two years the army told everyone I was a nut. I was ashamed. My mother and father was ashamed. Now they decided I'm very wise . . . without even testing me again. I ain't scared. Just show

me a soldier who'd like to be in that ring in my place."
After he had passed the physical examination, Ali refused to be taken into the Army. He said that joining the Army and fighting a war were against the Black Muslim Religion. Ali said, "I am dependent solely upon Allah as the final judge of these actions brought about by my own conscience." Later he said things like: "How can I kill somebody when I pray five times a day for peace," and "I don't know anything about Vietnam. Where is it anyway? Near China?"

The fight of his life was on. Ali was facing a $10,000 fine and five years in jail for refusing to go into the Army. Within hours of his announcement, the World Boxing Association announced that Ali was being

stripped of his championship title. This big fight was to go on for four years. The case was taken to the courts. Ali took his fight right up to the highest court in the land, the Supreme Court. Ali lost every round of this fight except the last one—the one that finally counted.

In an 8-0 decision, the Supreme Court cleared the former Heavyweight Champion of the World and ruled that he had been improperly drafted in the first place. Ali had won his fight with the Army but he still did not hold his title. During the legal fight, he had not stepped into the ring to fight as a boxer. But he had been doing other things during those forty-three months. He made TV commercials. He spoke before college students. He appeared in a Broadway musical. He kept making jokes and writing poetry. He said, "I can joke because I'm not going."

Ali's lawyers forced the World Boxing Commission to reverse itself and once again Ali could fight in the ring. Ali said, "I've already said a long prayer to Allah, that's my celebration."

The years away from the ring had cost Ali millions of dollars and he was asked if he would take legal action against those who had kept him out of the boxing ring. Ali said, "No. They only did what they thought was right. That was all. I can't condemn them for doing what they think was right." February 1970: Ali announced that he was going to retire from boxing! He said his title should go to the winner of the fight between Joe Frazier and Jerry Quarry. In that same month Frazier fought Jimmy Ellis in New York and won. Frazier was the new World Heavyweight Champion. September 1970: Muhammad Ali announced he would return to the ring. He wanted his title back. He was back fighting but the old timing and speed weren't there as they had been. He was still a great fighter but

the years of not fighting showed. October 1970: Muhammad Ali returned to the ring. He fought Jerry Quarry in Atlanta. Ali was a little slower but a lot stronger—and he won in the third round. December 1970: Muhammad Ali vs. Oscar Bonavena in New York City. The fight went into the 15th round. Ali let loose with a left hook and decked Bonavena. He decked him again and again. Ali won. It was the first fight Oscar Bonavena had ever lost of his 54 fights.

Ali was really after Joe Frazier, the man who held his crown of Heavyweight Champion of the World. As Ali put it, "I want Frazier." And again: "I want Frazier, NOW!" Ali wanted to prove he was world champ again so he could be "an ordinary citizen." He said he could then cut the grass and not be in the papers anymore.

Finally, March 1971, Ali faced Frazier in a fight to the finish.

The fight was fifteen rounds. Without question, it was the Fight of the Century. These fifteen rounds were to decide who was "the greatest" and the "onliest champ." Frazier had 23 knockouts (K.O.) in 26 consecutive victories. People said getting hit by Joe "is like getting run over by a bus." Ali had 25 K.O.'s in 31 straight wins. People said of Ali, "He moves like silk, hits like a ton." The public wanted to see this fight. In the first five weeks after the announcement of the fight between Ali and Joe Frazier, all the tickets were sold out at Madison Square Garden in New York City.

It was an important fight for Ali and he had the fight planned completely in his mind. Ali had more at stake than just his heavyweight title. Some people were unhappy about Ali's behavior. They didn't approve of his Muslim Religion. They felt he was against white people, they thought he talked too much. They didn't know about the time he spent signing autographs, for

BOWERS SCHOOL LIBRARY
Santa Clara Unified School District
Santa Clara, California

21

hours, for white kids outside his training camp. Or about the trips he took the time to make to visit children in the hospital. Ali said, many times, "We don't hate the white man. We just hate the way he treats us." Ali wanted black people to be proud of being black. "Angel food cake is white—devil's food cake is black, naturally," he had said. Black is good is the message he wanted to convey.

Ali put a lot on the fight when he said, "I'm not just fightin' one man. I'm fightin' a lot of men, showin' a lot more of 'em here is one man they couldn't conquer. My mission is to bring freedom to 30 million black people. I'll win this fight because I've got a cause. Frazier has no cause."

Before Ali stepped into the ring with Frazier, as he stood in front of his mirror, Ali could see it this way: "Bap! Bap! Bap! I jab him once, twice, three times. Dance away. I move in again. Bam. Bam. Bam. I get him again. He's movin' in, ain't reachin' me because he's too small to reach me." Ali was thinking: "I'm gonna add one more page (to boxing history) and then they'll close it up. Gonna be no boxing after me!"

But Ali was wrong. Very wrong. At first, Ali was the boss in the ring. He teased Frazier. He tried to make him nervous. So it went for almost five rounds. Then Joe Frazier looked at Ali, dropped his hands, and

asked Ali to please hit him. Ali jabbed him twice and Joe Frazier laughed. It was as if Frazier was telling Ali, "You can't hurt me. Even when I put my hands down, you can't hurt me." Frazier had said, before the fight, "I just let him go on talkin' to his own self."

In the sixth round, Frazier pushed Ali into the ropes. Frazier hit Ali again and again. In the eleventh round it looked as if it were over for Ali. But Ali went on and on into the fifteenth round when Frazier let go with a left hook that nearly took Ali's head off his neck. Ali was stunned. When Frazier remembered that punch, he said "He can sure take a punch. I hit him with a few from way down in the country."

Ali agreed with Frazier. "He tagged me with his best punch. But I had to get up. I kept thinking of all those people watching me, hoping and praying for me." Ali did manage to get to his feet and to finish the fight. All the fight judges agreed—Frazier had won. In spite of his plans—Ali had lost.

Ali had lost the fight but not his spirit. He said "I lost a fight, that's all. I'm going to have to make the best of it." Ali admitted his loss to Frazier. But he was also cheered up by the people who still admired and loved him. "People cried when I lost," Ali said. "But I won't cry. I have a responsibility to take a defeat like a great man. Any great man must know how to

conquer his defeats so the masses can conquer theirs. There are many upsets in life, and it is the wise man who can cope with them and inspire others to do the same." And he added, "Anyway, Frazier is a nice fella. He's got a family, nice kids. He's another brother."

After losing the second Frazier fight Ali also lost his chance to take the world title. He would have to fight other boxers before he could take another turn at the title for Heavyweight Boxing Champion of the World. Ali fought five exhibition games and worked out a lot. He would get another crack at Frazier. He was not one to give up. His fighting spirit was still very much alive.

July 1971: Ali next fought Jimmy Ellis, his former sparring (practice) partner. Dancing around the ring with style, Ali snapped Ellis's head back with a string of left jabs. In the remaining fifty seconds of the last round, Ali was declared the winner on a TKO.

But Jimmy Ellis was only a stepping stone to Ali. "Life is full of pressures," said Ali, "I still got a lot of work to do. If I could just wind this whole thing up, take my title back from Frazier, go on home and say 'whew,' and quit." Ali kept fighting exhibitions and matches all over the world—South America, Texas, Japan, Germany, Canada, Ireland, Maryland, Massachusetts, New York.

In the meantime, Joe Frazier was fighting too. And he kept the world title for a while.

March 31, 1973: a 31-year-old Ali stepped into the ring to fight a young twenty-eight year old boxer. The boxer was not well known. His name was Ken

Norton. Norton had never before fought a boxer as good or as popular as Muhammad Ali. Everyone, even Norton's friends, thought that Norton would quickly lose to the fast and furious Ali. But in the first round, Norton hit Ali in the jaw. Ali bled a little from the mouth. As the fight went on Ali got slower and slower. Norton looked very quick. Ali kept circling Norton throughout the fight. But Norton never left enough room for Ali to really get at him.

Near the end of the fight, Ali knew that he had better knock Norton out or else he would lose. In the last six minutes, Ali tried very hard. Ali's good boxing habits were there. He blocked, moved and jabbed as always. But he couldn't seem to get at Norton to deliver the big blow that would end the fight. Ali could not trap the 210 pound Norton. And so, Ken Norton, the former sparring partner of Joe Frazier, won the decision over Muhammad Ali.

In the meantime, Joe Frazier sat near Norton's corner. When Ali lost to Norton, Frazier was happy and broke into a huge smile. His biggest enemy in the ring, Muhammad Ali, had lost to his sparring partner! The crowd was not happy though. They were sad because they knew that the boxing career of Muhammad Ali was probably over. This fight marked the beginning of the end for Ali.

When the fight was over and Ali was declared the loser, he went to his dressing room. He sat there banging his head and his fists against the wall. He refused to see anyone including the newsmen who clamored to get in. Ali's trainer, Angelo Dundee, said to the newsmen: "I wanted to stop it in the second round but Ali wouldn't let me. The Boxing Commission doctor told me he had broken his jaw." Ali had no comment.

Not too long after Ali's loss Joe Frazier had some hard luck too. The new Heavyweight World Champion is a 25-year old man named George Foreman.

Defeated, but not broken, Ali has a life outside the ring which is full and rich. He has three daughters by his second wife. He is a millionaire. He lives in a mansion in Philadelphia. He writes. He acts. He is an important social figure. He has earned the respect of important people—black and white. But what will he do next? Are we to believe what he said after one of his fights, "I just want to sit one day and be an ordinary citizen. Go to the hardware store, cut the grass. Don't be in no more papers, don't talk to nobody, no more lectures. Just rest." That is certainly one side of Ali.

There is the other side of Ali, too. The side that doesn't like to lose. Ali—"the onliest" champ. The fast talking poet-fighter. Will he try to make another comeback? Will he try to regain his lost title, the title that was unfairly taken away from him? Only time will tell. But there is one thing for sure—whatever he decides to do, many people will always think of Muhammad Ali as "the greatest."

3 Indy Wins

CREATIVE'S
SUPERSTARS

Mark Spitz

Jackie Robinson

Johnny Bench

Wilt Chamberlain

Joe Namath

A. J. Foyt

Arnold Palmer

Bill Russell

Tom Seaver

Billie Jean King

Vince Lombardi

Roberto Clemente

Jack Nicklaus

Jerry West

Bobby Hull

Muhammad Ali

O. J. Simpson

Hank Aaron